Little Rainbow Rosary

Rose Maria Dennis
Illustrations by Terry Herb

Jesus said, "Let the little children come to me, and do not hinder them, for the kingdom of heaven belongs to such as these."
Mt. 19:14

© 2009 by Rose Dennis

Published by
Bezalel Books
Waterford, MI
www.BezalelBooks.com

Printed in the United States of America

All rights reserved. No part of this publication may be reproduced, stored in a retrieval system, or transmitted in any form or by any means—for example, electronic, photocopy, recording—without the prior written permission of the author. The only exception is brief quotations in printed reviews.

ISBN 978-0-9821222-7-3
Library of Congress Control Number

To my daughter Gabrielle L. Dennis: You are my inspiration and my heart, mommy loves you forever!

To Father Jim Brown: Thank you for opening up the door to the beauty of the Catholic Faith.

To Peggy Alexiou: Thank you for your inspiration.

This book is also lovingly dedicated to the Blessed Mother Mary who encouraged children in Lourdes and Fatima to pray the rosary.

~~~

A beautiful inspirational story, *Rose's for Our Lady*, by Georgia Alexiou, inspired me to research the meaning of the word 'rosary'. This led me to discover the writings of St. Louis De Montfort on the devotion. Through praying the rosary myself, and reading scripture, I realized this devotion is a glorious way to exercise God's greatest commandments. These ideas culminated in my decision to write a children's book on the topic. It is my hope that each child who hears this story will be blessed with an early love of God and interest in the beautiful rosary.

Gabriella was a little girl with a very big heart. She went to a school called Our Lady of Lourdes in Ohio. She liked school because she had a very nice teacher and several special friends.

When school was out, Daddy would help her with homework. Afterward, they would play soccer. She loved playing soccer because she could run really fast. Every time she kicked the ball in the net, her heart skipped a beat and she would give Daddy a high five!

Nighttime was always special for Gabriella and Mommy. Gabriella would curl up with her favorite teddy bear while Mommy tucked her in and read her a story from the Bible.

As Gabriella drifted off to sleep, she would see Mommy praying near the nightlight, holding her special blue beads with the cross.

One day, Gabriella asked Mommy when she would have her own special prayer beads.

Gabriella's Mommy smiled and told her that the beads were called a rosary. A rosary was something that Gabriella would learn step by step. "Are you ready to begin?" Mommy asked.

"Yes," Gabriella eagerly responded.

"Do you know what prayer is? When you say a prayer it is like telling God, 'I love you.'"

Gabriella thought of the prayers she learned in school.

"I'm supposed to love God with my whole heart!"

"Yes, that's God's greatest wish: love God with all your heart, soul and mind."

"That's a big prayer!"

"Yes, it is!" Mommy said and gave Gabriella a big hug.

Gabriella's mommy promised her that she would receive her first rosary when she learned to pray two important prayers: the Our Father and the Hail Mary.

"Will my rosary be blue like yours?" Gabriella asked.

"You may have any color that you want," Mommy said.

Gabriella had so many favorite colors that she couldn't make up her mind. Then, she looked at the picture on the wall of Noah's Ark and the rainbow. "I would like a rainbow-colored rosary!"

For days, Gabriella practiced the Our Father and Hail Mary prayers. Sometimes she could not think of the next word. Sometimes she had to ask what a word meant. But before long, Gabriella could say both prayers perfectly.

The very next night, Mommy took out a special gift-wrapped box and gave it to Gabriella. Gabriella was so excited that she skipped around the room. When she opened it, she found a beautiful rainbow-colored rosary! It was small and felt so comfortable in her hands. It had a cross, one yellow bead, and 10 multi-colored beads. Mommy called it a "decade" rosary. Her mother asked her to read the words on the back of the cross. It said, "To Gabriella, Love, Mommy." Gabriella was so happy that she drew and colored a special picture on the box.

That night Mommy told Gabriella that she was ready for the second step. Her Mommy taught her that the word **rosary** meant **crown** or **bouquet of roses.**

"Each time we ask Mary to pray to Jesus on our behalf, it's like giving a heavenly rose to Jesus, our Savior, delivered through His mother," mommy said. "In this way the Hail Mary shows love and humility. It also honors our mother Mary. When we say the complete rosary, we are giving a crown of roses to Mary and Jesus in heaven."

Gabriella thought this was so beautiful. She begged, "Mommy, let's say the rosary right now. We can make Jesus happy."

So Mommy held Gabriella on her lap and said, "We start by reading a story first, called a 'mystery'."

"What is a mystery?" asked Gabriella.

"A rosary mystery is a story about Jesus that you think about while you pray," said Mommy.

Gabriella asked, "Can Teddy Bear listen to the story and pray, too?"

Mommy smiled and said, "It would be better for Teddy to just watch." Mommy read a story about Jesus' birth.

Next, using the beads to count, Gabriella and Mommy prayed the Our Father prayer on the first bead, then one Hail Mary on each of the ten multi-colored beads. As Gabriella touched the different colors, she imagined that with each bead, she was sending colorful roses to Mary for Jesus.

After Gabriella learned that prayer was a way to show her love for God, Mommy taught her how to use prayer to honor God's second greatest wish. "Gabriella, when we pray for other people, we love our neighbors as ourselves."

As Gabriella grew, she prayed more rosary beads and learned more prayers of the holy rosary and its mysteries.

One day she learned to pray the complete rosary like her Mommy.

She always remembered God's greatest commandment: "Love God with all your heart, soul, and mind."

And she knew the second commandment, too: "Love your neighbor as yourself."

In that spirit she prayed the rosary for many people and thus showered heaven with roses of love.

Luke 18:13-14

"But the tax collector stood at a distance. He would not even look up to heaven, but beat his breast and said, 'God, have mercy on me, a sinner.'

"I tell you that this man, rather than the other, went home justified before God. For everyone who exalts himself will be humbled, and he who humbles himself will be exalted."

Hail Mary, full of grace.
The Lord is with you.
Blessed are you among women,
and blessed is the fruit of your womb, Jesus.
Holy Mary, Mother of God,
pray for us sinners,
now and at the hour of our death.
Amen.

Write your own note to Jesus

Dear Jesus,

_____
_____
_____
_____
_____
_____
_____
_____
_____
_____
_____

Love,